I Just Didn't Want to Say Goodbye

How to heal after losing a loved one

Hedieh Samimi

North Star Success Inc.

I Just Didn't Want to Say Goodbye:
How to heal after losing a loved one

ISBN: 978-1-9995333-4-2

of trade or otherwise, be lent, resold, or hired out or otherwise circulated without the author's prior consent in any form of binding or cover other than that in which it is published.

This is a work of non-fiction. Any resemblance of names, personal characteristics and details of people, living or dead, is coincidental and un-intentional. The author is solely responsible for the content of the book. The author's intent is only to offer information of a general nature to help you in your quest for emotional, physical, and spiritual well-being. The author of this book does not dispense medical advice and the reader is solely responsible for their actions and results.

Published by North Star Success Inc.

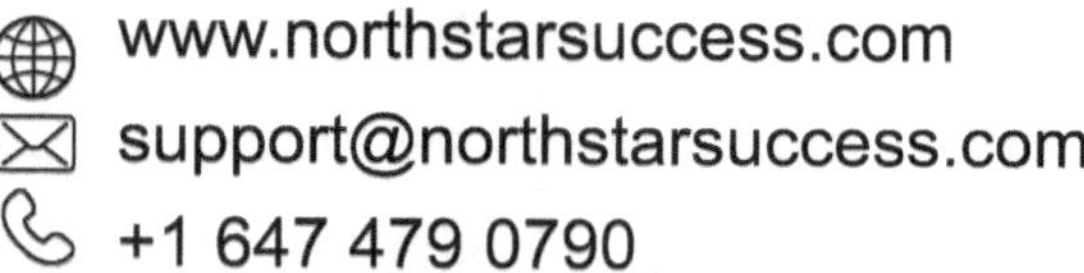

www.northstarsuccess.com

support@northstarsuccess.com

+1 647 479 0790

CONTENTS

Foreword by Dr. Shahab Anari

On January 16, 2009, several shells hit Dr. Izzeldin Abuelaish's home in the Gaza Strip, killing three of his daughters and a niece. But it was his response to the loss of his children that made news and won him humanitarian awards around the world. Instead of seeking revenge or sinking into hatred, Izzeldin called for people around the world to stop hating and start talking to each other[1].

You may think Izzeldin is an exception to the rule. 'Normal' human beings would have their heart shattered to pieces, hold deep grudges toward the other party, and try to retaliate at the first opportunity. However, Izzeldin is not a

____

1-https://www.nsb.com/speakers/dr-izzeldin-abuelaish

single example. Every single day, we see people who choose to cope, heal and thrive boldly despite the terrible pain of losing a loved one.

Then the key questions is: How can one go about bouncing back from the loss of a loved one?

This is what this book is all about. The author has personally experienced loss of a younger sister (to cancer) firsthand. She has also had extensive experience in coaching grieving people get over the pain and become complete with their loss. She is not only certified as a grief recovery strategist but she also has developed her own techniques that she has used successfully with her clients during the past few years. She shares her story along with actionable advice on how to do grief 'right' in this book.

Loss comes in many forms and instances. Loss of a loved one, divorce, immigration, moving, starting school, leaving school, loss of trust, and so on. However, to deliver a practical formula, Hedieh chooses to solely focus on 'death of a loved one' in this book. However, you can use the concepts and techniques presented in this book in other cases of loss as well.

There are so many misconceptions and myths around the concept of grief that makes grieving people suffer unreasonably. This book rectifies those false beliefs and sets out a plan to recover from grief with high awareness and open eyes.

Shahab Anari, M.D., CPC

Best-Selling Author, Featured on the Wall Street Journal as 'Master of Success'

I Just Didn't Want to Say Goodbye

How to heal after losing a loved one

Hedieh Samimi

Chapter 1
HOW IT ALL STARTED FOR ME

"I can't tolerate the pain. My tummy is terribly swollen. I need to get back to Toronto RIGHT NOW." This was what my little sister, Haleh, told my parents agonizingly on the phone while she was away with her husband on honeymoon in Italy. She didn't know then, though, that her abdominal pain was actually a devastating cancer eating her from inside.

I was living like a princess before I first found out Haleh had bowel cancer. My family had always been financially well-off and involved in charitable causes, like building schools in under-privileged districts. As sisters, Haleh and I were so close to each other that sometimes people mistook us for twins. Although Haleh was my baby daughter, she was considered the 'wise' kid in the family. In 2015, after having finished my MBA degree in Atlanta University in Dubai, we started SR Pay (a financial merchant service just that allows small business owners charge their customers' credit cards hassle-free) in Toronto, Canada. I was the founder and marketing manager, and Haleh was in charge of the financial management. Despite all the gruelling challenges and fierce competition, we managed to grow the business considerably in a relatively short time.

On February 14, 2015 we were at a party when Haleh made that dreadful phone call to my parents. She was away with her husband on honeymoon in Italy when the pain struck. Apparently, she had had the stomach ache for a few days and it had gradually become so unbearable that she simply couldn't stand it any more. Mom and Dad didn't take Haleh's complaint too seriously because she had always had similar episodes in the past due to her underlying chronic disease (Inflammatory Bowel Disease) and the pains had always gone away after a short while. However, Haleh insisted that it was different this time, and she needed to get back to Toronto asap. Therefore, she immediately got on a flight to Toronto, unaccompanied by her husband, who went back to Poland to continue his studies as a medical student.

I was away in Montreal for a dance competition that day, but Mom, Dad and Haleh's in-laws went to the airport to pick her up. What they faced at the airport made them both surprised and shocked. Haleh arrived pale and anguished, with a tummy so swollen that some even thought she might be pregnant. But that was an impossible explanation. So, everyone was wondering, "What was wrong?"

She was taken straight to the Emergency Department of North York General Hospital (NYGH) in uptown Toronto where she underwent several preliminary blood tests. The first-line diagnoses were either ectopic pregnancy or a normal flare of IBD (inflammatory bowel disease), which were ruled out over the next few hours. The extensive tests and biopsies that were done overnight at the hospital that night all alluded to the fact that Haleh's distended abdomen could be a sign of pre-cancer. Our family had previously been a business partner at a cancer-diagnosis lab in the Sunnybrook Hospital in Toronto, so we somehow had the knowledge and connections to perform some extra tests and get second opinions. Therefore, we took a sample of her biopsy to Sunnybrook, got an immunohistochemistry test done on it and asked some of the best doctors over there for their opinion. Also, the doctors at NYGH performed a colonoscopy on Haleh to see what was going on in her intestines. Unfortunately, everything pointed to just one diagnosis: high-stage colorectal cancer.

I vividly remember what happened when the NYGH doctors finalized the doomed diagnosis and told us that Haleh had just 5 months left to live. Fear spread among the members of my family like wildfire. Haleh started crying like crazy; Mom began screaming from the bottom of her lungs; Dad became so confused that he chain-smoked maybe a full packet of cigarettes non-stop. Except for me. I was in an utter state of denial and shock. I simply couldn't believe what I had heard. I thought there must have been a mistake, and even if Haleh had cancer, there would definitely be a cure for it, and she would recover from it fast. I kept telling everyone, "Haleh has had a bowel disease for the past 15 years. Everyone always told her that it would lead to cancer, but it never did. This time is the same. The symptoms will go away soon. She's going to be fine."

No matter how strongly I denied the seriousness of Haleh's condition, it didn't change the fact that she needed treatment for her cancer.

That was why the doctors began chemotherapy sessions for her, which was repeated every two weeks. Haleh's life gradually went back to normal, and except for a small percentage of time when she felt really exhausted or down, she continued living life just like a normal person.

Everything went very smoothly until the final chemotherapy session was done at Sunnybrook. That final session caused an intestinal obstruction, which means 'treatment failure' from a medical perspective. In other words, there was no hope for any cure, and Haleh's time was going to be over soon. The doctors told us, "We can't do anything else for you here." They then sent a priest to her room, who asked her if she had written her will. We were all dizzied by what was going on, and it was then that Haleh said, "Take me to Mayo Clinic, please. They can fix me up."

Dad arranged an air ambulance to take Haleh to Mayo Clinic in Phoenix, Arizona the same night. Mom, her mother-in-law and I got plane tickets for the next day (Dad couldn't accompany us because of visa issues, but he later joined us as well). Before we got on the plane, Dad pulled me aside and told me in private, "My dear daughter, Hedieh! We will have very difficult days ahead of us. You need to be strong, and you need to take care of your Mom. Know that there is a very small chance that Haleh will come back to Toronto ever again. Be prepared for anything" I acted cool just like nothing was going on. Not that I was stupid; I just couldn't believe what was happening. I was in mere denial. At the time, I thought this whole thing would take just one month, and Haleh would be cured in Mayo Clinic and we would all go back home in no time.

The first responses we got from the doctors at Mayo Clinic were encouraging. They said they might be able to help, and Haleh could even be a candidate for HIPEC (which is a highly concentrated, heated chemotherapy treatment delivered directly to the abdomen during surgery). At Mayo Clinic, I slowly became more and more involved with Haleh's doctors and began doing whatever I could to help her get the most out of her treatment. The doctors kept telling me, "If she wants to get the HIPEC treatment, she needs to get physically and emotionally strong, and you are the person who can help her get there." That was why I constantly tried to walk her around the hospital to build up her stamina, talked to her positively to motivate and inspire her and keep up her spirits, and even played piano at the common space so that she could enjoy the sound of music and feel better again.

I kept telling her, "Look, Haleh, cancer is a disease. You could become cancer-free just like the lady next door. You just need to keep up your fighter spirit, do your art therapy, and hope for the best. Everything is going to be fine." I even asked the art therapy instructor at Mayo Clinic if Haleh could teach painting to the other patients there (since Haleh was an artist herself), which she agreed to happily. I literally did everything I could ever think of to help boost her morale and physical vigor.

The intestinal obstruction wasn't going away and that was why after a while, the doctors gave up trying and decided to stop the chemotherapy treatment. They said, "It's best to release Haleh from hospital because there was nothing else we could do for her." We negotiated with the hospital authorities to keep Haleh in hospital during her final days, however. A few days later, Haleh passed away silently in my Dad's arms.

For another year, I was still in utter shock and denial, and acted as if nothing serious had happened. However, something happened that eventually broke me down and smashed my life to pieces. Almost one year after Hale's passing and only 10 days after my wedding, my ex-husband sent me a voice message saying that he didn't want to live with me anymore. This blow shook me so hard that the landslide finally came down. After such a long time of living in mere denial, I suddenly experienced the life-shattering impact of two severe losses: Haleh's passing and break-up with my ex-husband. I went into a deep state of depression, feeling lonely to the core. I now began to truly realize that Haleh was REALLY gone for good and there was no coming back. I began going to therapy sessions, where my psychologist reminded me that I had just started going through the natural grief cycle; a cycle that should have started quite a while before but, in my case, had been delayed until now.

During those dark moments, I locked myself up in my room, and cried my eyes out all day. I just wanted to go to sleep and never wake up, since sleep was my only escape from the terrible pain

I was going through. I even made two suicide attempts, but every single time, I heard Haleh's voice ring in my ear, "Hedieh! Do not do that. There are people out there who need you. You have a mission to accomplish. You need to finish what I couldn't finish in this world."

Not only did Haleh save my life in those two cases, but she also appeared in my dreams in another instance and asked me to go talk to my ex-husband and finish off everything with him on a clean slate. Although this move was impossibly difficult for me, I pulled myself together and finally did it, and I confess it absolutely transformed my life. The mere feeling of forgiveness that I experienced after talking to my ex-husband released me from all the bad feelings I had been holding onto for quite a while.

I opened up to new possibilities after that, which has been bringing me new opportunities consistently ever since. With the help of my life coach and good friend, Mitra Mohamadzadeh, I got certified in NLP and even started incorporating music therapy and art therapy in my coaching practice. I also got certified as a grief recovery specialist, and I started helping people who were going through situations similar to what I had experienced.

The story of Haleh's painful passing led me to where I am today. My life completely changed as a result, and I started helping more and more people in my practice: Haleh Alchemy Coaching[2].

And I couldn't be any happier.

2-I learned most of the concepts I have presented in this book in my Grief Recovery Certification program, and all the credit of this methodology goes to the Grief Recovery Institute. Visit their website here: https://www.griefrecoverymethod.com.

Hedieh's
photo

Haleh,
Hedieh's
sister

Chapter 2

Grief, It's All Natural

What is grief, exactly?

Grief is the natural and normal response of a human being to a loss. There are a few keywords in this definition. First, there's a 'loss' involved:

- death of a loved one
- divorce
- immigration
- major health changes
- retirement
- etc.

Although every single one of these instances are important in their own right, I'm going to be focusing on the first definition of grief in this book (i.e. loss of a loved one).

Second, the response is 'natural and normal'. Grief is more than just an emotional reaction; it involves physical, behavioral, and cognitive responses as well. The key distinction here is that all the symptoms that someone experiences after the loss are absolutely normal and natural. Symptoms such as:

- feeling sad and heartbroken
- wanting to talk about the lost loved one
- feeling exhausted and depleted
- having low concentration
- feeling numb and senseless
- sleeping too much or too little
- eating too much or too little
- having extreme fluctuations of emotions

There's nothing wrong with shedding tears because you've lost a loved one. There's nothing wrong if you want to talk about it. There's nothing wrong if you keep thinking about that beloved person and your fond memories with them. There's nothing wrong about feeling choked when somebody mentions their name, or something reminds you of them. There's nothing wrong about any of these. It makes perfect sense to feel that way, and anybody in your situation would be like that.

Client Story in Their Words

It gives me tremendous relief to know that it's normal to have these feelings. It makes me feel finally at ease to know that I'm not defective. I've consistently felt uncomfortable with my feelings and emotions after my Mom passed away three months ago. There have been times when I wanted to talk to my friends about my Mom, but I suddenly got the feeling that this might not be right. I told myself, "After all, it's my problem and I don't need to ruin their day by flooding them with negative emotions and sad memories about my late Mom. I'd better get myself together and act as if nothing has happened."

Also, since I've been out of shape, emotionally speaking, I've been wanting to stay home and sleep instead of going out and hanging with my friends. Besides, I have been eating more than I used to and this has led to me gaining a bit of weight. I always thought this might be a sign that I'm getting depressed and I might need medication. But now I know that it might not necessarily be the case. And all of these are natural and normal responses to the fact that I've lost someone I loved so much.

However, the common reactions we get from well-meaning but ill-educated people around us are something along the lines of:

- Don't feel bad.

- At least, he's not in pain anymore.

- At least, you got to know him and spent 20 years of your life with him.

- I'll get you another dog.

- If you're going to cry, go to your room.

- Leave her alone. She'll be fine in a little while.

- Just give it some time.

- etc. *(more on this in the next pages)*

These kinds of reactions somehow imply to us that grieving is not the right thing to do; the griever needs to change his/her attitude because they are being ungrateful; grieving makes other people uncomfortable; and in brief, grieving is bad.

But I'm here to tell you, "Grieving is normal. Grieving is natural. And you have every right to be wanting to grieve."

We Are Not Prepared for Loss

We are not prepared for loss in our society. We are never taught how to deal with our emotions when someone we love dies. Neither are we taught how to behave toward someone who has lost a loved one. Maybe it's because losing someone close is not a very common happening in a person's life and that's why we don't face this challenge frequently enough to learn how we can handle it.

The problem has many facets. Many people just don't want to talk about death. Think of when a father dies, and the little child in the family asks, 'What happened to Dad?' No straightforward answer is given to such a child.

'He's gone to heaven'

'He's gone to sleep forever.'

'Dad is now with God.'

How is the child supposed to digest what exactly is going on?

Also, many people just feel awkward when it comes to expressing human emotions openly. Lots of people are not comfortable with crying or showing their pure emotions or being encountered with an individual who does so. And last but not least, many people want to give spiritual advice when a griever expresses his/her emotions. They might say:

'Loss is an opportunity for you to learn more about the philosophy of life. It's meant for spiritual growth, not crying.'

'Have faith. There's a meaning behind every-thing that happens.'

Unfortunately, anybody who has experienced loss firsthand knows that none of this helps.

Stages of Grief

Although you may have heard of the 5-stage grief cycle many times, I'd like to emphasize that there are no stages to grief after you've lost a loved one. David B. Feldman, PhD writes in his noteworthy article on Psychology Today[3], "Among the general public, one of the most commonly known and accepted psychological concepts is that grief proceeds in stages. If you already are familiar with the stages of grief, you have psychiatrist and visionary death-and-dying expert Elizabeth Kubler-Ross to thank for it. Through her many books and tireless ac-tivism, Kubler-Ross managed to change how much of the world thought about death. She

3-https://www.psychologytoday.com/ca/blog/super-survivors/201707/why-the-five-stages-grief-are-wrong

helped soften some of the stigma that had previously been present, making it a little more okay to talk about and get support for loss.

What you may not know, however, is that Kubler-Ross didn't originally develop these stages to explain what people go through when they lose a loved one. Instead, she developed them to describe the process patients go through as they come to terms with their terminal illnesses. The stages—denial, anger, bargaining, depression, and acceptance—were only later applied to grieving friends and family members, who seemed to undergo a similar process after the loss of their loved ones.

Grief turns out not to be so simple.

Studies now show that grievers don't progress through these stages in a lock-step fashion. Consequently, when any of us loses someone we love, we may find that we fit the stages precisely as Kubler-Ross outlined, or we may skip all but one. We may race through them or drag our feet all the way to acceptance. We may even repeat or add stages that Kubler-Ross never dreamed of. In fact, the actual grief process looks a lot less like a neat set of stages and a lot more like a roller coaster of emotions. Even Kubler-Ross said that grief doesn't proceed in a linear and predictable fashion, writing toward the end of her career that she regretted her stages had been misunderstood.

The unfortunate side effect of our society's erroneous but firm belief in the five stages is that many people wind up criticizing themselves for 'not doing grief right.' When people buy into the idea that there's only one healthy way to grieve, then it's easy for them to attack themselves when they naturally find that they're doing it differently. This kind of self-criticism never helps anyone."

So, remember: grieving is unique and individual.

Client Story in Their Words

It's both comforting and upsetting to hear that the 5-stage grief cycle is not universal.

It's comforting because I always thought there must be something wrong with me because I was not going through the stages in the correct order. As a matter of fact, I was not experiencing some stages at all. For me, there were no clear stages to my grief. It was just an extreme rollercoaster of emotions and hodgepodge of indistinguishable feelings that left me confused and exhausted.

On the other hand, it's upsetting to know this because there so many people who are ashamed of themselves thinking 'Why am I not going through these stages? Why am I not feeling anger, denial, etc? Is there something wrong with me? Am I grieving right?' It's so sad that these individuals not only suffer from the pains of the loss itself but they also experience the shame and embarrassment that goes with not going through the five stages.

Signs of Being Incomplete with a Loss

Most of the time, we are not even aware that we're not complete with our loss. We have lost a loved one and we think we are doing 'fine' getting over the terrible circumstances, but, in reality, there's something unresolved in that relationship. These are the common signs that might suggest you are not complete with your loss:

- You do not want to think about or talk about the deceased person.

- Your good memories of them are turning painful.

- You only talk about the positive aspects and attributes of that person.

- You only talk about the negative aspects and attributes of that person.

Client Story in Their Words

I now know that I'm still incomplete with the death of my younger sister. She died very unexpectedly in a car accident when she was driving to visit me one weekend. How do I know I'm still incomplete? Because whenever I talk about her, several things happen.

First, I tend to think of her as a 'perfect' human being. I now see that I exaggerate

how she was as a person, and I tend to just focus on the fond memories that we had together.

I also notice that every time I think of her, her memories quickly translate into a sad feeling inside my body. A feeling of being hollow and at the same time heavy. When I get that weird feeling, I just don't want to move at all. It's an overbearing feeling of sorrow and being depleted of energy all at the same time.

Chapter 3

Why Try to Recover?

Consequences of Not Recovering

I read in a report by *National Mental Health Association that* in the U.S. alone, 8 million people suffered through the death of someone in their immediate family in 2003; 800,000 new widows and widowers; 400,000 people under 25 suffered from the death of a loved one. Think about all these huge numbers. How staggering can the negative outcomes of unresolved grief be?

When a griever does not recover fully from their loss, a lot of potentially harmful consequences may ensue. Outcomes such as these:

- The griever feels so sad that their situation may be misdiagnosed as depression (or even ADHD or PTSD),

and, therefore, they will be mistreat-
ed due to having similar symptoms
while the real cause of the problem
has not been identified and dealt with.

Client Story in Their Words

For the longest time, I was treated with anti-depressants by my psychiatrist. The first few months after my husband died was unbearable. I did everything I thought might be helpful and surrounded myself with everything I believed would help me. All to no avail.

At first, I tried therapy. A friend of mine recommended a therapist she had used after her husband's death, who she said had helped her recover much faster than she thought possible. I tried therapy. I don't know what the problem was, but it didn't work for me. I personally thought the therapist was more interested in my childhood problems than the fact that I was suffering from my husband's passing.

Then, I asked my family physician to refer me to a psychiatrist. I was diagnosed as having severe depression and the specialist put me on an anti-depressant diet. I was on medication for three years. I felt a slight lifting in my moods, but the principal problem had been left untouched. Whenever I thought about my husband, I felt terribly down in the dumps and I couldn't help but breaking into tears. The situation had got so unbearable that one day I decided to stop taking the pills and try grief coaching as a last resort.

That was what led me to you. And I'm happy I made that call.

- The griever loses their energy and engagement with their daily tasks, resulting in diminished output at work and inefficient social interactions, which will eventually damage their professional and personal life in significant ways.

Client Story in Their Words

After I lost my wife to a sudden death, I just didn't feel like going to work. Most mornings, I felt I had no energy whatsoever to get myself out of bed and go to work. Even when I managed to go to work, I couldn't concentrate, and I felt like a zombie going through the motions of the day.

Obviously, with no passion and no concentration, my work suffered. I missed a few deadlines, and my output was way less than ideal. My clients began getting dissatisfied with my services, and one by one they canceled their accounts with me.

Soon I realized if I didn't do anything serious about my problem, I would be in a very bad situation in no time.

And that was when I started searching for help.

- The griever may succumb to ineffective strategies to help them cope with the problem; strategies that deliver short-term results but fail to address the core issue. Lots of grievers turn to consuming alcohol, eating too much food, doing too much shopping, engaging in sex, workaholism, and other vehicles only to distract themselves so they can feel less pain. These methods do have short-term value but will not help in the long run.

Client Story in Their Words

After my little sister died, I resorted to all kinds of things to get my mind off of the terrible pain of her loss. All those actions made me get out of whack physically, emotionally and financially.

I would eat too much, especially too much pastry, and I gained 30 pounds in less than a year.

I would go shopping and spend a lot of money on stuff, only to feel remorseful about what I had done the moment I got home. I remember during one of my trips, I spent $10,000 buying clothes at fancy stores, which made me go over my credit limit and pay a lot of interest in the end.

I would drown myself in useless meetings with unqualified prospects in my business, but although I was putting in a lot of work, nothing showed in the results. As a matter of fact, the bottom line was going down, and I was being drained emotionally at the same time.

Common Fallacies about Grief

I've always been amazed at why we are never educated on some very important subjects at school. To name a few, there are key subjects such as finances, communication skills, and, of course, handling grief. We are never taught what to do when we lose a loved one. The subject is awkward to navigate, and people tend to avoid it altogether. Just look at some of the biggest misconceptions and bad pieces of advice about grief that are prevalent in the society:

- *Time heals all wounds.* Of course, time alone is not capable of healing anything. Our 'action' over time is the defining factor. I've met individuals who have been experiencing the negative emotions of incomplete loss even 20 years after the incident.

Client Story in Their Words

Time does NOT heal. At least it doesn't heal the wound of a 'loss', I assure you of that.

I spent 8 years in an almost-depressed mood after I lost my son to cancer. Yes, I had the luxury of an ultra-supportive husband and close family nearby, but I can't say the pain wasn't there. I just had a strong support system who helped me go on every time I thought I couldn't take it any longer.

My son died of pancreatic cancer at the age of 36. I was 58 at the time. Most people say a 'normal' person will get back to their normal performance 6 months after the loss. Apparently, there was nothing normal about my case. The first year I just couldn't get back to work. This unfortunately led to me being replaced at work, and my original plans of retirement simply fell through. Now, I not only was dealing with the pain of losing my son, but I also had to cope with the fact that I now needed to look for another job.

The moment you think it can't get any worse, my husband passed away too. Three years after my son's passing, my husband died, which left me alone, shocked and confused. My family did a phenomenal job of holding my back when I downsized and went through all the tasks necessary to take care of the estate. But I felt I was permanently broken, and nothing would ever help me get back to my 'normal' state.

Time didn't heal my wounds. Each unre-solved grief just kept adding to the pile.

- *Keep busy.* Keeping busy provides only a temporary relief through creating distraction. We all know we may be able to distract our attention to a less painful subject by keeping busy, but does this strategy remove the underlying cause and prevent it from resurfacing in the future?

Client Story in Their Words

When I heard my best friend had died in a car accident, I was utterly shocked. A feeling of numbness overcame my body. I couldn't move, I couldn't speak, and I didn't know whether this was a terrible nightmare or the sheer truth. The first moments after I heard the news felt as if I was transported into another world. All the pictures and sounds around me became blurry and muffled.

The first few days was horrible. I sobbed uncontrollably. I was afraid to go to my friend's house because I was worried I might not be able to tolerate the whole emotional outburst. I could not imagine what pain her mom and dad were going through, and the thought of facing them crying their eyes out made me feel terrible.

Seeing that I was in a very bad place emotionally, people close to me, especially my parents, started giving me all kinds of advice:

o *Don't stay home. Go hang out with your friend.*

o *Play some piano. It will take your mind off of the loss.*

- o *Why don't we go to the movies to-gether?*

- o *etc.*

I resisted some of them and I agreed to some, but the truth is that these measures were just temporary. The moment I was finished with them, my mind quickly bounced back to her memories like a spring that had been pulled. Now I know the commonality among all these pieces of advice was 'distraction'. By resorting to them, I was just trying to divert my attention away from the pain without actually doing something to solve the problem.

- *Replace it.* A lot of good-willed friends and family members tell us to replace the loved one with a new alternative. They may say,

- o You can always have another baby.

- o I'll get you a new dog.

- o etc.

Despite having the best of intentions at heart, these people are not helping the griever cope with the loss that's hurting them.

Client Story in Their Words

I think what a griever needs MOST is to be heard. A griever doesn't expect anyone to be able to bring back the loved one from the dead. They don't expect others to solve an unsolvable problem. They don't expect anyone to be able to miraculously launch them to a happy emotional state.

They just want to be heard.

I remember when I lost my first baby five months into pregnancy, some of the most common sentences I heard from my family and friends were:

   o   *Don't feel bad. You can always have another baby.*

   o   *Be grateful that you're young and fertile.*

   o   *This was never meant to be.*

   o   *You'll never remember this happened. Your next child will fill your heart with love.*

Even though these were well-meaning utterances by good people, they were absolutely useless. Yes, I knew that I was young, and I could have another baby in the future, but still the pain was there. The possibility of having another baby was real, but how was I supposed to cope with the pain I was experiencing right then and there?

- *Be strong for others.* We as grievers are often told to get ourselves together and be strong for others around us who are less strong. For example, a grieving father who has lost a child might be told to be strong for his wife who is badly devastated. Although this sentence makes intellectual sense, the question remains as to how the father himself is going to cope with the pain.

Client Story in Their Words

I lost my Dad to cancer when I was 16 years old. This was an exceptionally unique experience for me in several ways.

First, I had never personally experienced the loss of a loved one before. I wasn't prepared for it, and I was lost and confused as to how I was supposed to behave.

Second, at the ripe age of 16, I was constantly told by others to be strong for my Mom and my little sister. I was the only 'man' in the house, and apparently I was expected to act normal and be the rock for my family. The problem was that I had never been in a similar situation before and I didn't have any instructions on how to do that.

Third, I was experiencing a rollercoaster of emotions myself, but since I was supposed to be strong for others, I just put on a false image of 'normal' and buried my feeling somewhere deep down.

I now know that by being strong for others, you might be helping them get through the pain, but you'll be neglecting your own needs to be heard and soothed.

- *Grieve alone.* Over time, we have been socialized to believe that it's just un-classy or childish to cry in front of others or to talk about a lost one. When somebody starts crying in a group, they are usually pulled aside so that they won't create an awkward feeling among others. Children are often told to leave grieving adults alone until they have got a hold of themselves emotionally. The key question is, how can an isolated griever overcome their problem when they badly need support and attention from people around them?

A Common Problem

Our society has a problem with expression of feelings. We see this everywhere:

o   In the corporate world, there's an unwritten code of manners that says, 'No expression of strong feelings such as loud laughter or crying.'

o   In schoolgrounds, kids label those who cry a lot as 'cry-babies'.

o   In parties, when kids start to cry, parents pull them aside and remind them how impolite and uncivilized their behavior is. They are told, "If you want to continue crying, we will have to go home."

o   Boys are continuously told, 'Men don't cry.'

I believe crying is a natural way of expressing one's feelings. If crying is bad or abnormal, why are human beings equipped with it in the first place? I think we are mistakenly socialized to believe that crying in front of people is not appropriate, and if we want to express our feeling in this way, we'd better find somewhere isolated and cry alone.

I believe that's why a lot of people choose to grieve alone.

All these misconceptions cause the griever to put on a mask and fake an "I'm fine" attitude while there's really nothing fine about their situation.

Completing is NOT forgetting

When I talk about being complete with a loss, I mean 'discovering and finishing' what was emotionally unfinished for you in your unique relationship with the deceased person. I do NOT mean that we are trying to find a way to forget the other person. What we are seeking is to

- feel better

- feel normal once again when you want to think about or talk about the lost loved one

- see the deceased person in a truthful light, including both their positive and negative aspects

By trying to be complete with the loss, we want to stop putting on a false 'recovered image' just to pretend to the world that everything's OK. We want to finish any unfinished communication with the loved one so that we can remember them in an honest light and cherish their memories without feeling bad anymore.

Client Story in Their Words

I must confess I was one of those people. For a long time, I thought if I went through the recovery process, I would be able to deal with the loss, but eventually I might forget my best friend of 30 years. I just didn't want to forget him. Therefore, I resisted the idea of recovery. I wanted to stay in the grieving mode.

I remember you asked me in one of our sessions, "Can a parent ever forget their child?" It was a simple question. I answered, "No, they can't." Then you pro ceeded to ask, "Then I'm not trying to help you 'forget' your best friend. I just want you to get over his death. I don't want you to be permanently sad whenever you think of him. I want you to be able to remember him, treasure his memories, and talk about him without feeling emotionally overwhelmed."

How to Become Complete with a Loss[4]

4

4- I learned this methodology in my Grief Recovery Certification program, and all the credit of this methodology goes to the Grief Recovery Institute. Visit their website here: https://www.griefrecoverymethod.com.

The right time to begin to recover

It's never too soon to start the process of recovery. A wrong common belief is that the griever needs to spend a specific length of time grieving before they are finally 'ready' to begin to recover. This can't be further from the truth. Actually, grievers are ready and willing to talk about the experience of loss and their relationship with their loved one immediately after the loss.

Client Story in Their Words

Some of the problem might be cultural. In my culture, the griever is somehow supposed to be extremely sad for an extended period of time. Actually, grievers are generally expected to show some of the reactions below in the first few weeks after the loss:

o   sobbing heavily

o   throwing themselves to the ground and repeatedly shouting the person's name in a loud voice

o   breaking out in tears whenever someone mentions the name of the deceased person

Therefore, neither the griever nor the people around them would think of immediate recovery as a reasonable idea. They implicitly believe that if you start the recovery too soon, it's a sign that you might not have loved the lost person enough. Or it might mean that you are just going through the motions, but, in reality, you are not sad that this person has passed.

I can tell you this: In my community, it's a frightening idea to even think about starting the recovery immediately after the loss.

The first step of the completion process

Success in the completion process is the result of small and consistent actions on the part of the griever. The very first thing you need to do to start the recovery process is to decide to take 100% responsibility for your thoughts, emotions, and actions. Please note that I'm not saying you can completely control what happens in your life. That statement would obviously be incorrect. My point here is that although you can't control the circumstances, you can AL-WAYS control your responses to those circumstances. To re-enforce this concept, I'd like to quote Jack Canfield on his famous formula:

$$E + R = O$$

where E = event, R = response, and O = outcome.

In other words, you can't control the E (outside event). If you want to change the O (= outcome), you need to change your R (= response). That's where you have absolute control.

On the one hand, taking full responsibility means to stop blaming others (including the lost loved one) for how you feel. You need to internalize the fact that 'they' didn't make you feel sad by passing away. 'You' were the one who had that response based on your interpretations of that event and how you went about reacting to it. If you want to acquire an empowering mentality that will help you get complete with your loss in the fastest possible manner, you need to get rid of the 'victim' mentality and start taking responsibility for how you feel. This is a difficult concept to swallow and we'll be talking about it more later on. On the other hand, taking full responsibility also means deciding to be brutally honest with yourself. More often than not, we tend to omit, minimize or maximize certain events because they're simply painful to do otherwise. If you want the recovery process to go smoothly and successfully, you have to be 100% honest about what you did or did not do, and you need to be truthful about who the departed person truly was without any exaggeration or distortion of the facts.

Client Story in Their Words

That's right. A big obstacle to starting the recovery process is the fact that grievers sometimes don't want to face certain truths.

In my case, my young daughter committed suicide when she was only 16 years old. I had noticed for quite a while that she was acting strangely, locking herself in her room for long hours. She sometimes said she didn't want to go to school anymore, and when I inquired why, she didn't give me a clear response. I confess I never tried to understand what was really going on. A few times, I tried to start a conversation with her at the breakfast table, none with any success.

I thought, "Maybe that's a phase she's going through. She might have problems with her boyfriend. Or maybe she's had fights with her girlfriends at school. She's just a teenager, and this is all too common among teenagers."

Obviously, I was dead wrong. I later found out by talking to her friends that my daughter was being bullied at school, and the situation had got so harsh that she just couldn't stand it anymore. My baby daughter might not have taken her life if I had been more attentive.

And this sense of guilt stopped me from starting the recovery process for a very long time. I just couldn't face the fact that I might have contributed to her decision for committing suicide.

Map the Relationship

What you need to do at this point is to take a detailed and complete look at your relationship with the lost loved one. In order to do this, use a sheet of paper (legal size or similar). Turn the paper sideways and draw a line across the middle of the page. The end left of the line represents the beginning of the relationship with the loved one. The right end of the line represents the current year. Positive or happy events are marked above the center line, and negative or sad events below the line.

To do this right:

- Be honest and thorough.
- Put at least two events above and two below.
- List the events no matter how big

or small they seem.

- Use the length of line to indicate intensity.

Take a look at the graph below as an example (this is the graph of a grieving client of mine who lost her little sister to cancer):

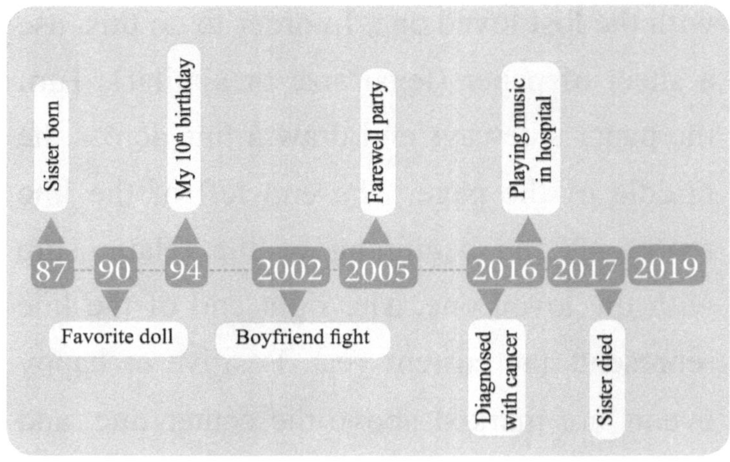

'87: My little sister was born. I was 4 years old then. My Mom and Dad had told me that I was going to have a baby sister. For this reason, I was so excited about the prospect of having a little sister at home whom I could play with. Of course, when the baby came home from hospital, I immediately realized she was too small to play with me. She couldn't even sit up straight. I was a bit bummed, but I was extremely happy that I got to be the big sister.

'90: My baby sister broke the arm of my favorite doll while she was playing with it. I was really mad. I had told her several times that I didn't want her to play with that specific doll, but she kept ignoring me. One day, she threw the doll down the stairs from the second floor and broke the doll's right arm. Although Dad tried hard to fix it, he couldn't. I was pretty rough on my little sister and made her cry.

'94: On my 10th birthday, my parents threw a big surprise birthday party for me at home and invited all my friends with their family. I got a lot of gifts and was over the moon with joy. But the most beautiful gift I received was a scrapbook my little sister had created for me. She had put the pictures of me and all the people who mattered to me (my Mom and Dad, my friends, my favorite teacher, my dog, etc.) in it. She had also written on it: "I LOVE you. From your little sister."

'2002: One day, my boyfriend, my sister and I went out to movies together. My boyfriend started kissing me in the dark of the movie theater. My sister thought it was so gross and she couldn't handle it. She left us and went home. When I got back home that night, I had a fight with her because I thought she had embarrassed me in front of my boyfriend. We began a cold period in our relationship after that incident.

'2005: In 2005, I got admission in a B.A. program in economics from a university in another city which was 3 hours flight away from home. My parents threw a farewell party for me and invited family and friends to it. At some point, my little sister came and sat beside me.

She hugged me and said, "I know we sometimes don't get along together. Just wanted to tell you that I love you and I'll miss you." I knew she loved me, but it was great to hear it, anyway.

'2016: In 2016, I had got back to my hometown and was working in a local bank there. My sister had had unusual symptoms in her gastrointestinal tract, such as bleeding and bloating, for almost a year when her GI doctor announced to us after a colonoscopy that she had intestinal cancer. It came as an unexpected blow to all of us in the family, particularly when we found out it was a high stage cancer.

My sister was soon hospitalized because we couldn't take care of her at home anymore. Her health deteriorated rapidly, and doctors told us that she had only a short few months left. I quit my job at the bank and dedicated myself to caring for her and being with her during her last months. One day, I tried to get her out of bed and take her for a walk in the hospital. She was so weak that she wasn't able to do it. Therefore, I went to the common area close to her room, sat at the piano that was sitting there, and played one of her favorite pieces. When I went back to her room afterwards, she was in tears. This was a very touching and proud moment for me.

'2017: My little sister died after being in a coma for 2 weeks.

Now, it's your turn. Do your Relationship Graph here.

Client Story in Their Words

I had a hard time doing the Relationship Graph. I was going to do it for the miscarriage of my first child. At first, I didn't know exactly how to define the end left of the line. You said I needed to define it as the moment I got pregnant with the baby. Then I tried to fill in the details, but my memory wandered. I didn't know where to start. With your help, I realized it didn't matter to go in chronological order. I figured that I could go back and forth as long as I recalled everything and jotted them down. Sometimes, I just cut out some events because I considered them as insignificant, but you kept telling me not to edit or limit myself. At times, I felt stuck and I couldn't think of any event to put on the graph. At these moments, I went back to the example graphs you provided (like the one above) and got inspiration.

It took me about an hour to complete the graph.

Turning the Graph into Actual Recovery Statements

After you've mapped out the graph, you need to complete the recovery process by writing sentences conveying 'apology' for things you did wrong to the deceased person, 'forgiveness' for things that they did wrong to you, and any other 'strong feeling' that you have for them (feelings such as love, hate, pride, appreciation, etc.)

The intention here is to get complete with un-finished communications. The unfinished emo-tional businesses are the root of all unresolved losses, and by following the above instruction, we tend to put an end to any such emotion. It doesn't mean that after this process, you'll nev-er get sad or you'll never need to talk about the loved one. It only means that things will get back to normal, and you will feel 'complete' because you have expressed all of those unex-pressed feelings.

A little note about forgiveness: Remember, for-giving the other person is not about you being wrong or them being right. The other person may have done really bad things to you, and there might be no doubt about it. The reason why I recommend you forgive them is that you don't want to carry that burden all your life. You let go of the bad feeling and you CHOOSE to set yourself free because you deserve to be calm (not because they had any right to behave the way they did). This is a very important distinction.

Based on the sample Relationship Graph provided above, the Recovery Statements can go as follows:

o   I want you to know that I was really happy and excited when you were born.

o   I forgive you for breaking my favorite doll's right arm.

o   I apologize for being rough on you for breaking my doll.

o   I apologize for not telling you at my 10th birthday that your scrapbook was the best gift I received that day.

o   I forgive you for your insensitive

behavior toward me and my boyfriend at the movies. I got really embarrassed that day.

o I'm sorry I didn't take the time and energy to remind you how much I loved you, even though you did so several times, especially at my farewell party.

o I'm really sad that you didn't notice your symptoms early enough to be able to prevent the cancer from progressing into high stages.

o I'm proud that you appreciated me playing the piano for you in hospital.

o I'm really sad that I didn't get to know you more and share happier memories with you.

Client Story in Their Words

When I wanted to convert the Relationship Graph into Recovery Statements, I had a hard time forgiving my loved one. I thought he was to blame for the things he did, and I just didn't want to forgive him. But you told me that any resistance on my part would mean the retention of the resentment. And who was going to be harmed by that? Well, me (he was gone and he couldn't be bothered, literally).

You emphasized that forgiving has nothing to do with the other person. You said, "It's a choice you need to make. Do you want to set yourself free or not? You can't feel forgiveness until you decide to do it. You need to forgive first, and then you'll feel the difference it will make in your emotional state. Just give it a try. You'll be doing it for yourself."

Now, it's your turn. Write your own recovery statements based on your Relationship Graph.

In the Grief Recovery Handbook, John W. James and Russel Friedman advise that the griever write a Completion Letter by putting together an actual letter that compiles and lists the Recovery Statements. They suggest the griever group the statements by category, write the letter and finally read it to a partner[5] whom they are working on their grief with. Here's a formula you can follow:

Dear.........(name or title that best represents person)

I have been reviewing our relationship, and I have discovered some things that I want to tell you.

........., I apologize for......

........., I apologize for......

---

5   The partner can be anyone, but someone who has experienced emotional loss is a better option. A good partner will be honest, will promise to hold everything in absolute confidentiality, and won't judge you.

.........., I forgive you for..........

.........., I forgive you for..........

.........., I want you to know..........

.........., I want you to know..........

.........., I love you, I miss you ..... OR .... I have to go now.

Good bye.

Here's an example of such a letter based on the sample Relationship Graph above:

Dear little sister H.,

I have been reviewing our relationship, and I have discovered some things that I want to tell you.

H., I apologize for being so rough on you for breaking my doll.

H., I apologize for not telling you that your scrapbook was the best gift I received on my 10th birthday.

H., I'm sorry I didn't take the time and energy to remind you how much I loved you, even though you did so several times, especially at my farewell party.

I forgive you for breaking my favorite doll's right arm.

I forgive you for your insensitive behavior toward me and my boyfriend at the movies. I got really embarrassed that day.

I want you to know that I was really happy and excited when you were born.

I want you to know that I'm really sad that you didn't notice your symptoms early enough to be able to prevent the cancer from progressing into high stages.

I want you to know that I'm proud that you appreciated me playing the piano for you in hospital.

I want you to know that I'm really sad that I didn't get to know you more and share happier memories with you.

H., I love you, I miss you.

Good bye.

Some final tips:

- Writing is best done alone and in one session. It normally takes between 30 minutes and one hour.

- This part of the process can be painful. Don't let the pain stop you from going the last mile of the journey.

- The letter can be of any length, but the average letter is between 1 and 2 pages.

- Always end with 'Good-Bye'. This is a goodbye to the pain, and it brings closure to the task.

- It's worthwhile to remember that

when you have recovered, it's perfectly normal to feel sad from time to time or want to talk about the lost loved one with those around you.

- After you've written the Completion Letter, whenever you remember sad memories, just try to replace them with the fond memories you have of the loved one. You have lots of memories of the departed person. It will be your choice in the moment to choose which memory to focus on.

- If after writing the Completion Letter, you find out there are still unresolved communications left, don't worry. You can always add Recovery Statements to your letter and read it to a reliable partner.

- Before anniversaries and birthdays, get prepared. Don't try to do it alone. Isolation is never helpful.

- After you've done the whole process, you can go back and focus on other losses that you may have experienced before and repeat the process to get complete with them as well.

Bonus

What to Say and What NOT to Say to a Griever

What NOT to Say to a Griever

- Don't feel bad; his suffering is over now.

- It's just a matter of time. You'll be fine.

- You're young; you can still have other children.

- It was just a dog, cat, etc.

- I know exactly how you feel.

- This is taking too long. Why are you feeling that way still?

- At least, they're in a better place.

- At least, you got to know him and spend a few years with him.

What to Say to a Griever

The most helpful thing you can say to a griever is something that lets them feel heard. The best way to do this is to ask questions, stay curious, and then acknowledge and validate their feelings. Although there are not fixed magical phrases for this situation, you can always use sentences like these:

- What happened?

- Tell me more.

- So, what did you do next?

- You have every right to feel that way.

- Anyone in your situation would feel that way.

- I can't imagine how you feel.

- I can't imagine how painful that must have been for you.

- So, what you're saying is that ….

Listening well is the key to having an effective conversation with a griever. If you focus on 'them' and what 'they' are saying (not what YOU think is appropriate, or what has happened to 'you' in similar situations), you'll be good. A great way to achieve this is to be present and focused in the moment and stop all judgment or criticism. Be as empathetic as you can be, and try to see and feel the world through the lens of their eyes.

Hedieh Samimi's

Programs

Coaching:
Grief Recovery

I've always been eager to understand my own and others' motivations and behaviours.

Understanding grief and loss on a personal level (losing my only beloved sister & husband) has driven me to pursue NLP Coaching and Grief Recovery so that I might be of service to those challenged by the painful experience of losing a loved one.

The goal of my coaching program is to help YOU learn and to encourage YOU to mourn well.

Workshop: Should I Stay or Should I Go?

It is one of the most common questions that I get from my clients who are agonizing over their relationship, desperately wanting to make the right choice and wishing they had a crystal ball to foresee the future consequences of their decision.

This Workshop is filled with life changing information that will be a great help to anyone who joins it. No matter what stage of a relationship you're at, there is something in this workshop for everyone.

You will learn a set of powerful tools, strategies and guidelines that you can use to make this life-changing decision as clearly, positively, and confidently as possible.

You can contact me at:

https://www.halehcoaching.com

info@halehcoaching.com

416 988 5280

9 781999 533342